Perception

By
Faith Brynie

Scientific Consultant:
Dr. Paul Thompson
Assistant Professor of Neurology, UCLA

BLACKBIRCH PRESS, INC.
WOODBRIDGE, CONNECTICUT

Published by Blackbirch Press, Inc.
260 Amity Road
Woodbridge, CT 06525
Web site: http://www.blackbirch.com
e-mail: staff@blackbirch.com
© 2001 Blackbirch Press, Inc.

Printed in Belgium

10 9 8 7 6 5 4 3 2 1

Photo Credits:
Cover, back cover, pages 11, 14, 16, 20, 39 (top and center), 40, 44, 48, 50, 55, 60: PhotoDisc; pages 4, 6 (right), 35 (bottom), 37, 39 (bottom), 59: Corel Corporation; pages 6 (left), 22, 26, 29–30, 53, 56: Blackbirch Press, Inc.; pages 10, 12–13, 17–18, 24–25, 32–33, 42, 45, 54: LifeArt; page 27: courtesy Faith Brynie; page 28: ©Photo Researchers, Inc./Omikron; page 49: courtesy Ellen Covey.

Library of Congress Cataloging-in-Publication Data
Brynie, Faith Hickman, 1946–
        Perception / by Faith Brynie.
                p. cm. — (The amazing brain)
        Includes index.
        ISBN 1-56711-423-7 (hardcover)
        1. Senses and sensation—Juvenile literature. 2. Perception—
Juvenile literature. [1. Senses and sensation. 2. Perception.] I. Title. II.
Amazing brain series.
QP434 .B794 2001   00-012022
573. 8'7—dc21   CIP
                                                                           AC

Table of Contents

Chapter 1

Brain Alert!

A lion sniffs the wind. Wildebeest are grazing nearby. The lion follows the scent, crouching low in the savanna grasses as its prey comes into view. The predator lies in wait, until one grazer—old and weak—wanders from the herd. The lion's muscles coil, poised for the pounce.

On another continent, evening falls over a pond. Frogs rustle the reeds and perch on water lilies. Under cover of approaching darkness, a male puffs out his membranous throat and advertises his location with a mighty croak. Soon others join in, until the marsh rings with the animals' pulsing chorus.

In a fifth floor apartment in a large city, a human mother cradles her baby in the crook of her arm. She strokes the child's pudgy cheek and hums softly as the infant sleeps.

What do the stalking lion, the croaking frog, and the adoring mother have in common? Although the settings and the behaviors differ, each is responding to information in the environment. Neurons (nerve cells) in their sense organs are sending data to their brains, whether about the smell of prey, the failing light, or the touch of a sleeping infant. Their brains, in turn, interpret that information and send impulses to nerves in the muscles, which stimulate movement or action.

Though it is difficult to notice, there is another similarity among the three examples. In each setting, the subject's brain is filtering out irrelevant sensory information. The barks of hyenas from a distant ridge do not distract the lion. The frog croaks, despite water splashing and insects buzzing nearby. The human mother ignores traffic noises from the street below, the smells of cooking in the next apartment, and the scratch of her wool sweater against her skin. These animals are unaware that automatic "decisions" and interpretations are constantly being made in their brains—sometimes thousands every minute.

The "decisions" can change in a heartbeat. Any change in the environment can cause a shift in nerve impulses, brain activity, and behavior. The lion backs off when humans appear. The frog falls silent the instant an owl is heard. And, should the mother

Animals sense and react to the world as their brains receive data from neurons all over their bodies.

smell smoke, her brain will react instantly—sending her dashing for the fire escape clutching her startled infant.

Sensing and Perceiving

The scent of a wildebeest is unlikely to set you on the prowl. Twilight will not provoke you to croak like a frog, either. As silly as this may sound, these examples make a good point. The meaning of sensory input depends on whose brain is processing it. In the brain of a male frog, dusk triggers a mating call. In a human brain, it is more likely to prompt the flipping of a light switch.

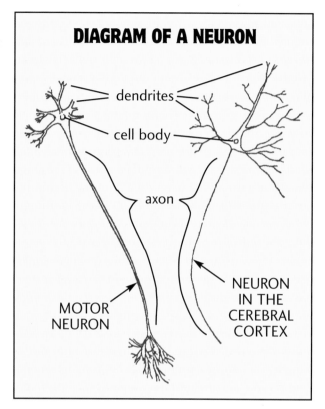

DIAGRAM OF A NEURON

dendrites

cell body

axon

MOTOR NEURON

NEURON IN THE CEREBRAL CORTEX

Scientists, therefore, recognize a difference between sensing and perceiving. Sensing involves unprocessed data. Light entering the eye falls on the retina. Molecules in the mouth and nose come in contact with taste buds and olfactory (smell) receptors. Sounds set the eardrum vibrating. These are sensory input from the environment.

Perception is more than sensing. It is processing, interpreting, and reacting. It is the conversion of sensory information into nerve impulses that the brain receives, assesses, and acts on. Perception is active, not passive. In humans, it turns nervous stimulation from the senses into "experience." For example, the odor of a wildebeest probably will not make your mouth water, but the aroma of apple pie fresh from the oven might. In both instances, nerve impulses and brain action have sifted, organized, and given meaning to chemical information. The wildebeest smell means little to you. The apple pie means potential satisfaction.

Humans are not the only animals that sense, perceive, and act. Cockroaches, for example, have mushroom-shaped structures on top of their brains. These cup-shaped parts receive signals from the eyes and other sense organs. In turn, the mushroom structures send signals to the brain centers that control behavior. Cockroaches use visual landmarks to find their way around, but when researchers cut the connection between their mushroom organs and the rest of the brain, they get lost—even though their vision is normal.

Perception is basic to learning. German researchers trained honeybees to stick out their tongues in response to certain odors. The bees' reward was sugar water. The behavior, however, was also taught without the sweet treat. Electrical or chemical stimulation of neurons in the brains worked just as well.

The Senses

Human senses gather data on up to five environmental variables:

- light, or the visual sense
- sound, or the hearing (auditory) sense
- chemicals, perceived as smells (the olfactory sense) or taste (the gustatory sense)
- pressure and temperature, or the sense of touch (including the perception of pain)
- gravity, or the sense of balance, position, and movement through space

Although these senses vary in many ways, their basic mechanisms are the same. From sensory nerves in the eyes, ears, skin, and other sense organs, messages travel from all parts of the body to the brain. Information travels as a series of nerve impulses. An impulse, simply, is a change in the electrical current that travels along the membrane (wiring) of a neuron (nerve cell). The change comes about because, when a sensory stimulus creates an impulse, channels in the cell membrane open and close, allowing charged atoms to enter and leave the cell.

Neurons in sense organs begin firing (carrying impulses) when stimulated by a change in the environment. For example, certain cells in the retina of the eye—called rods—initiate nerve impulses when the intensity of light changes. Rods contain a pigment called rhodopsin. Light actually changes the shape of the rhodopsin molecule, which stimulates an impulse. This impulse travels from the rod through the optic nerve to the visual centers of the brain. There, the significance of the impulse is assessed. Sunlight is discerned from shadow. Combined with other visual information, the form, hue, and size of an object are judged.

Changes in the environment need not be external. Internal chemical sensors involve neither taste nor smell, but their functioning is vital to survival. For example, in humans, the carotid body (at the branch of a major artery of the neck) responds to changes in the amount of oxygen in the blood. When the level falls, neurons emit an impulse. The signal travels to the respiratory centers of the brain. There, it stimulates neurons that send signals to the chest muscles. Their accelerated contractions speed the rate of breathing and increase the oxygen level in the blood.

Brains Respond

In humans and other animals with backbones, nerve fibers (bundles of axons and dendrites) are centered in the spinal cord. They act as a communication network.

Twelve pairs of cranial nerves descend through the base of the skull and extend to the face, sense organs, heart, and lungs. These cranial nerves include the auditory nerve that brings messages about sounds from the ears and the optic nerve that carries impulses from the eyes. Below that, 23 other large pairs of nerve branches carry impulses from the skin, muscles, joints, and body tissues to the brain.

Nerves also carry messages in the opposite direction—from the brain to organs and muscles. The impulses that travel through motor (movement) neurons cause muscles to contract. Some motor neurons control actions that are automatic and unconscious, such as salivating in response to the smell of apple pie. Other motor neurons trigger voluntary action, such as dashing to the kitchen to get a piece of apple pie.

The brain also communicates chemically. For example, the hypothalamus in the human brain detects changes in the sugar level of the blood. When the level falls, the hypothalamus releases chemicals that bring on feelings of hunger. When blood sugar rises, the hypothalamus sends the "I'm full" signal to the stomach and other parts of the body.

Hormones are chemicals that are made in one organ but affect another. Hormones made in the brain initiate physical responses and behaviors throughout the body. The interplay of hormones and nerves can produce complex responses. The mother's bond to her child, for example, involves hormones that trigger physical responses such as milk production. Her hormones also bring on emotional states, such as love and contentment. These biological reinforcements to mothering are not just about feeling good. They have evolved in animals—especially mammals—to increase the chances of survival.

Brain Terrain

Regions of animal brains each specialize in the kind of sensory inputs they process. We assume that these same regions also each specialize in the perceptions they create. In the croaking frog, for example, vision is centered in the large optic lobes of its midbrain. The front of its brain specializes in the sense of smell. But, in the lion, odors

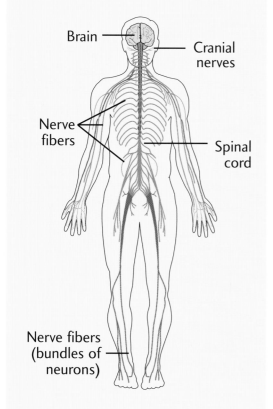

Electrical impulses in neurons send messages to the brain. Nerves are made up of many neurons.

THE CENTRAL NERVOUS SYSTEM

Brain

Cranial nerves

Nerve fibers

Spinal cord

Nerve fibers (bundles of neurons)

It Pays to Pay Attention

"Every second, we get millions or hundreds of millions of bits of information coming in from our senses," says Johns Hopkins scientist Ernst Niebur. "And we have to decide, every second, which part is important and which is not."

To find out how the brain makes such decisions, Niebur and his colleagues studied brain activity in monkeys. The animals had to focus their attention while identifying a lighted square going dim on a video monitor or comparing the shapes of raised figures pressed against their fingers.

When the monkeys paid attention, neurons working on the task increased their rate of all firing at the same time (called synchronous firing). Niebur thinks that messages sent in unison allow the brain to pick one item out of the flood of incoming information. Just exactly how attention actually increases synchronous firing remains a mystery.

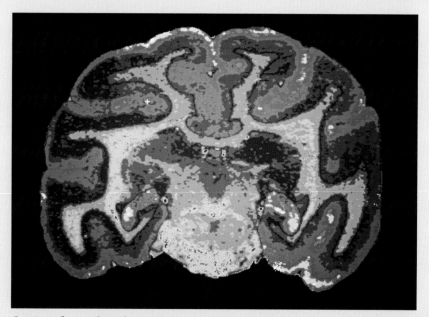

Section of a monkey's brain, shown in an enhanced PET scan.

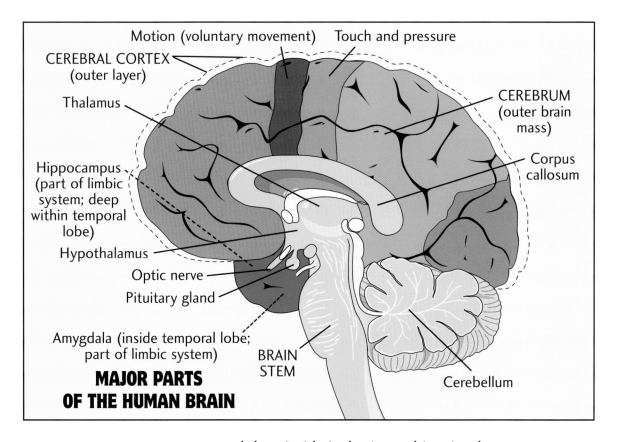

Motion (voluntary movement)   Touch and pressure

CEREBRAL CORTEX
(outer layer)

Thalamus

CEREBRUM
(outer brain mass)

Corpus callosum

Hippocampus
(part of limbic system; deep within temporal lobe)

Hypothalamus

Optic nerve

Pituitary gland

Amygdala (inside temporal lobe;
part of limbic system)

BRAIN STEM

Cerebellum

**MAJOR PARTS
OF THE HUMAN BRAIN**

are processed deep inside its brain, and its visual centers are closer to the surface.

In the human brain, a region called the thalamus serves as a kind of relay station. The thalamus passes impulses from all the senses—except smell—on to the cerebral cortex. (The cortex is the thin layer that covers the outside of the cerebrum.) The thalamus sorts important impulses from insignificant ones. It creates perceptions of hot, cold, pain, and pressure. The thalamus also plays a role in memory, which may explain why foods and songs can bring back vivid recollections of past emotions or experiences.

Also linked closely to sensory processing is the limbic system. The limbic system lies above the cerebellum, which is the brain area that coordinates posture, balance, and movement. The organs of the limbic system play a part in regulating body temperature, blood pressure, heart rate, and blood sugar. Two parts of the limbic system, the hippocampus and the amygdala, are essential to forming memories.

The limbic system is also the center of human emotions. Has a familiar scent ever evoked a vivid—but unexpected—memory? If so, was that memory a very happy or a very sad one? If you have felt that connection, you have experienced the ability of the limbic system to link sensory data with emotions and memories.

Most sensory processing occurs in the cerebral cortex. A strip of cortex across the top of the brain is the major processing area for touch. The principal motor (movement) processing area lies just in front of it. Other brain centers interpret input from other senses. The primary visual areas lie at the back of the brain, above the cerebellum. Sounds and smells reach centers on the side of the brain above the ears.

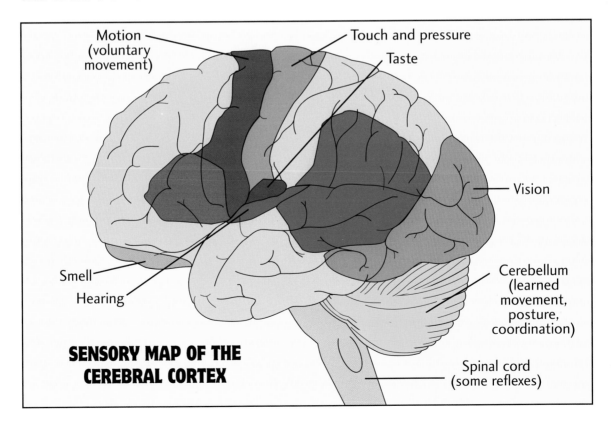

SENSORY MAP OF THE CEREBRAL CORTEX

Chapter 2

Touch

Can you tell a stuffed rabbit from a real one with your eyes closed? Of course. Your sense of touch tells you immediately that one is warmer, softer, and more flexible than the other.

Beneath the skin of your hand lie some 100,000 nerves of more than 20 kinds! Eight types are motor nerves. They cause the muscles of your hand to contract. Another twelve kinds specialize in responding to particular stimuli. They fire an impulse when they encounter pressure, heat, cold, vibration, or any of several kinds of pain. They send the following four kinds of information to the brain:

- What is it? Most neurons respond to only one kind of stimulus, such as heat or cold.
- Where is it? The brain knows where an impulse comes from. Different nerves carry messages from the hands, back, toes, and other sites.
- How strong is it? The more nerve endings that are stimulated—and the faster they fire (up to 1,000 times per second!)—the stronger the impulse.
- How long is it lasting? When a stimulus stops, the nerve impulse stops. It will also stop if a stimulus continues for too long. For example, you can wear a watch all day without noticing its pressure after the first few minutes.

Receive and Transmit

Every sense depends on structures called receptors. Receptors are specialized neurons that fire only in response to a specific stimulus. Receptors that are sensitive to light are found only in the eyes. Sound receptors are localized in the ears. Touch is different. Its receptors occur all over the skin. Some especially sensitive parts of your body have a huge number of receptors crowded into one place. A postage-stamp-sized patch of your hand contains some 134 yards (or 124 meters) of nerves that terminate in about 9,000 nerve endings!

Some touch receptors are free, or open, nerve endings. They occur in large numbers around the roots of body hairs. When air moves across the skin, it moves the hairs and triggers impulses in the free nerve endings. Free nerve endings also send pain signals.

Another kind of touch receptor is structured like a capsule that contains jelly-like material and a neuron. When the capsule is squeezed, the jelly slides across the neuron and initiates an impulse. Encapsulated neurons, especially numerous in the fingertips, fire in response to pressure or vibration. Another type of capsule receptor pinpoints the location of a stimulus.

Fingertips are especially sensitive to touch—each contains more than 3,000 touch receptors! Fingernails are dead tissue and contain no receptors, but the skin beneath them does. Those receptors are sensitive to impact. They generate nerve impulses when the fingertips strike any surface such as a piano key.

Fingertips are one of the most touch-sensitive parts of the body.

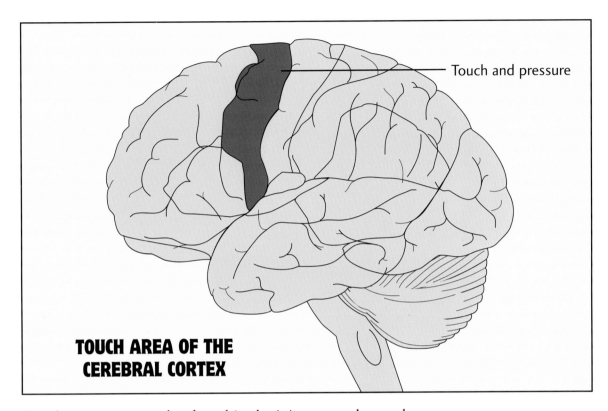

Touch and pressure

TOUCH AREA OF THE CEREBRAL CORTEX

Touch receptors are also found in the joints, muscles, and some internal organs. They fire when joints bend, muscles flex, or damage to tissue provokes pain. Receptors in the membrane that surrounds the stomach respond to the pressure of a big meal or the pain of food poisoning.

Touch signals that occur on the body's left side actually travel directly to the right side of the brain, and vice versa. The thalamus directs such impulses to the touch area at the crown of the head. Another structure, the hippocampus (a part of the limbic system), helps the brain "decide" whether to ignore an impulse or to act on it. The hippocampus compares impulses second by second. If an impulse does not change—such as the consistent pressure of a watchband—the hippocampus orders the brain to ignore it. If an impulse is new or different, the hippocampus alerts the cerebral cortex.

If a response is ordered, impulses travel to the motor cortex. This area lies close to the touch area of the brain. It orders the muscles in the needed area to contract, and the body responds in the appropriate way—such as scratching an itch or rubbing a sore muscle.

Pain

One scientific researcher estimated that an average single square inch of human skin (6.5 cm^2) contains only 165 nerve endings for touch, but a whopping 1,300 for pain. That may be because different pain receptors respond to different pain stimuli. For example, one kind of receptor signals cuts, and another kind signals burns.

Pain begins when damage or disease causes pain receptors to fire. The speed at which the impulses travel varies according to the type of pain. A pinprick impulse travels about 98 feet (30 meters) per second. A burn or ache travels much more slowly, about 6.5 feet (2 meters) per second. Nerve fibers carry the impulse to the spinal cord and then to the thalamus in the brain. The thalamus sends the pain message on to the cerebral cortex, initiating the awareness that something hurts. The impulse also travels to the limbic system, where emotions such as sadness, anger, or anxiety become associated with the pain.

Injured cells release chemicals that boost the pain signal and initiate the body's defensive response. One group of pain-response chemicals is the prostaglandins. They increase the flow of blood

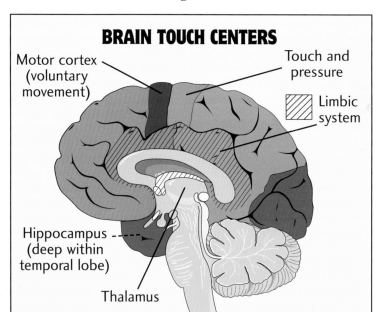

BRAIN TOUCH CENTERS

Motor cortex (voluntary movement)

Touch and pressure

Limbic system

Hippocampus (deep within temporal lobe)

Thalamus

to the injured area. That increases the number of infection-fighting cells (white blood cells) that travel to the site. Prostaglandins also increase the sensitivity of nerve endings to pain.

In some cases, your body can respond to pain before your brain becomes aware of it. For example, touch a sharp object and you will pull away an instant before you realize you have cut your finger. This kind of reaction is a product of something called the reflex arc—a direct connection between sensory and motor neurons through the spinal cord. The motor nerves trigger immediate muscle contraction. Further damage is avoided more quickly than if the command had to first travel all the way back from the brain.

All touch receptors, including those that fire when cells are injured, work like switches. They can be on or off, but nothing in between. So how does the brain tell a major injury from a minor one, at least in terms of pain? The greater the number of receptors stimulated, the greater the pain.

Heat and Cold

An average square inch (6.5 cm^2) of skin contains 78 receptors for heat and 13 receptors for cold. It also contains 65 hairs (most too tiny to see) and tiny muscles attached to those hairs. Hot and cold receptors help keep healthy body temperature at a steady 98.6° F (37° C). In a chilly room, the skin's cold receptors fire, sending signals to the hypothalamus in the brain. The hypothalamus responds with messages back to the skin, causing tiny blood vessels to expand and bring more heat to the surface. The impulses also cause the hair muscles to contract. The hairs rise and create a layer of dead air space that reduces heat loss from the skin. This response is more effective in furry animals than in relatively hairless humans.

The opposite happens in response to heat signals. If enough heat signals are sent to the hypothalamus—as they are on a hot day or during exercise—the brain sends messages to the tiny muscles around the sweat glands. The muscles contract and force perspiration out through the pores. The liquid evaporates on the skin's surface, taking excess heat with it.

Heat and cold receptors are specific in their response. When researchers stimulate a cold receptor with a warm probe, the subject feels only cold. Stimulate a heat receptor with a cold object, and the subject feels warmth. However, a heat receptor stops firing at extremely high temperatures. That's when pain receptors take over. The same happens at temperatures that are cold enough to cause tissue damage with frostbite.

A World of Touch

Which of the senses is most important to your survival? Human beings can live, work, and play without hearing or vision. They

can thrive on tasteless food and get along without smelling the roses. But touch is essential to life itself.

Put your hand too near the fire and heat receptors send the message, "Danger!" Your body reacts immediately, saving you from injury or death. Feeling pain or discomfort is essential to surviving. Most infants and toddlers do not need to be burned more than once to learn the danger of fire.

Of all the senses, touch is the one that makes us most "human."

Touch is also a form of communication that is as essential to humans as breathing. No words are needed to explain a gentle kiss or a caress. Hostile touches trigger the body's stress chemicals, those that prepare it to fight or run away. Gentle

Pattern Recognition

Use school glue or thick paint to make a capital "B" on paper. When it dries, blindfold some friends and ask them to recognize the letter by touch alone. Chances are they will do so easily, despite its similarity to other letters made from vertical bars and half circles.

Your brain recognizes the letter "B" even with all its possible variations.

The human brain is a master at pattern recognition. It ignores minor differences and tunes into similarities. Johns Hopkins researcher Kenneth Johnson and his team want to know how the brain is so good at doing this. Working with monkeys, they have found that—for a fraction of a second—the pattern of nerve impulses exactly matches the form of the letter. Neurons preserve information on the shape, size, and orientation as impulses travel through the nerves of the hand, arm, and spinal cord to the thalamus. But as soon as the impulses reach the touch lobes of the cortex, some kind of coding occurs. The brain separates the inputs, ignoring some and attending to others. In the cortex, the "B" is perceived as a "B" no matter what the variation.

"The image must be stored in memory," Johnson thinks. "The brain must compare it with others and say 'Aha! That matches!'" How are such coding and uncoding achieved? "That's the intriguing question," Johnson says.

touches slow a rapidly beating heart and stifle the release of stress chemicals into the blood. The sense of touch bonds a parent to a child within moments after birth. Studies have shown that infants deprived of touch fail to thrive. Those that are touched often, and with love, do the best.

Touch informs the brain of much more than the nature, site, strength, and duration of a stimulus. It also shapes our emotions and molds our social interactions. In many ways, touch is a big part of what makes us human.

Smell and Taste

L ife offers two basic choices. One is to approach. The other is to avoid. For most animals, survival depends on selecting correctly. Taste and smell are our chemical detection senses. They allow animals—including human beings—to find clean air, pure water, and safe food. Smell is essential to the survival of populations as well as individuals. Odors mark territories, advertise mates, and allow family members to recognize one another. They signal friend or foe, and inform whether to approach or flee.

The Sense of Smell

Of all the senses, smell is the brain's most direct link with the environment. Molecules floating in the air dissolve in mucus inside the nose. There, they stimulate some 100 million smell receptors of 1,000 different kinds. (That is far more than are used for color vision or taste.)

Molecules in the air trigger impulses that race along the olfactory nerve to the olfactory bulbs of the limbic system. Unlike all the other senses, smell impulses do not then travel to the thalamus. They go instead directly to the olfactory center in the brain's cortex. That's the special place where odors are identified. Smell signals also travel to the hypothalamus, the brain region that regulates the body's master gland, the pituitary. Through their effect on the hypothalamus, smells can influence appetite, emotion, sleep, and much more.

People with a good sense of smell can recognize as many as 10,000 different odors. How? The nose does not contain a

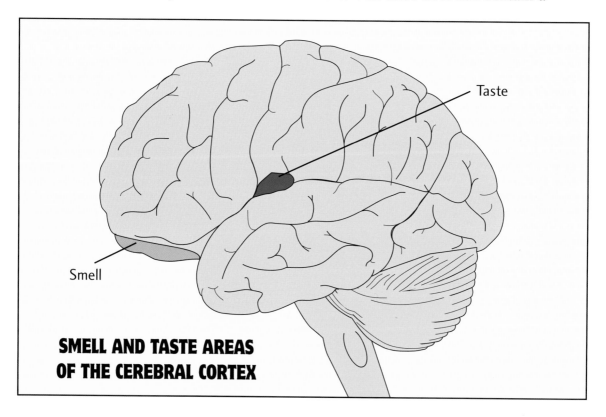

Taste

Smell

**SMELL AND TASTE AREAS
OF THE CEREBRAL CORTEX**

different receptor for each kind of odor. Scent receptors respond to part of a molecule's structure, not to the entire molecule. That means different molecules may stimulate some—but not all—of the same receptors. The brain identifies odors by evaluating patterns of impulses. Very simply, imagine that burning rubber stimulates receptors A, B, and C. Burning wood stimulates B, C, and D. Your brain distinguishes the two because the combinations are different.

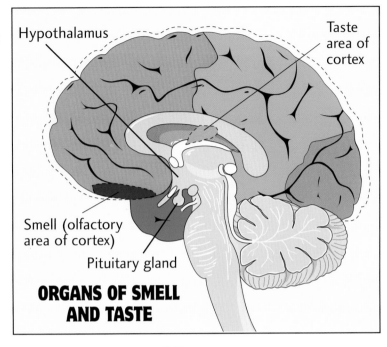

Hypothalamus

Taste area of cortex

Smell (olfactory area of cortex)

Pituitary gland

ORGANS OF SMELL AND TASTE

The brain's olfactory, emotion, and memory-forming centers in the limbic system lie close together. Perhaps that is why odors are so good at bringing back memories. They may also be powerful triggers for behavior. For example, scientists let asthmatic children smell vanilla every time their asthma medication was administered. In time, their lung functions improved without medication when they simply smelled vanilla.

The Sense of Taste

Hold your nose and chew a slice of onion. Do you notice a slightly sweet taste and a crunchy texture? Now release your nose. Suddenly, you know it is onion! Chewing releases molecules that travel up the back of the throat into the nose. Although taste and smell are processed in different areas of the brain, much of what we call flavor is actually smell. For every one molecule of a substance that can trigger a smell impulse, it takes 25,000 to initiate a taste impulse.

Some 10,000 taste buds lie on the tongue's rough surface. Some taste buds also line the palate and throat. About a dozen taste cells operate inside each taste bud. Tiny hairs protrude from each neuron through an opening in the bud called the taste pore. The saliva in your mouth bathes each hair. When food enters your mouth, some of its molecules dissolve in your saliva. When the molecules stimulate the taste hairs, the neurons generate chemicals called "second messengers." (The food molecules are the first messengers.) Second messengers change the taste cell's electrical charge. A nerve impulse begins.

Without much success, scientists have tried to associate the shape, size, structure, electrical charge, or atomic weight of molecules with their taste. For example, investigators have found that bitter substances increase the amount of a second messenger called IP3, but how IP3 produces the perception of bitterness remains unknown. Another second messenger is called cyclic AMP. Taste-testing laboratory mice cannot taste without it, but just how cyclic AMP works is a mystery.

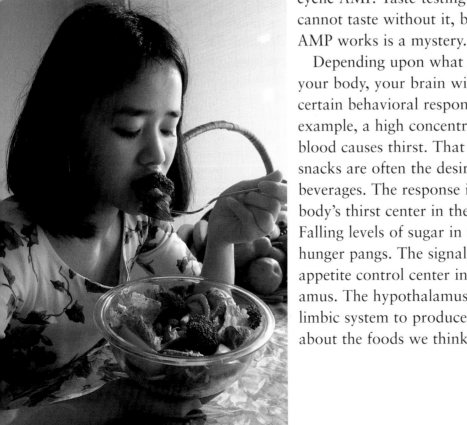

Taste buds react to five kinds of stimuli—sweet, sour, bitter, salty, and umami (MSG).

Depending upon what is happening in your body, your brain will also order certain behavioral responses to food. For example, a high concentration of salt in the blood causes thirst. That is why salty snacks are often the desired mix with beverages. The response is triggered by the body's thirst center in the hypothalamus. Falling levels of sugar in the blood trigger hunger pangs. The signals come from the appetite control center in the hypothalamus. The hypothalamus also acts with the limbic system to produce strong feelings about the foods we think we love or hate.

Of Hot Peppers and Pain Killers

If you love hot peppers, your affection is really for a chemical called capsaicin. Capsaicin binds to heat receptors and produces the spicy hot taste of peppery foods. The receptor detects temperatures between 110° and 120° F (43–49° C.). That is hot enough to burn! The capsaicin receptor also contributes to the perception of pain. Heat and toxins released from diseased or injured tissues activate the chemical. Protons (positively charged particles released from the nuclei of atoms) from damaged cells bind to capsaicin, lowering the temperature at which heat becomes painful. Some researchers think that if a drug can be developed that can block the capsaicin receptor, the drug might someday be mass produced and used to relieve pain.

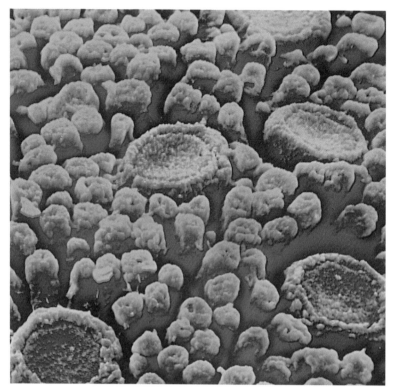

This magnified photo of the human tongue's surface reveals some of the 10,000 taste buds (highlighted in purple) that detect sweet, sour, salty, bitter and umami.

Taste buds react to five kinds of stimuli—sweet, sour, bitter, salty, and umami (MSG). Also, the brain's interpretations are affected by receptors in the mouth that react to temperature, touch, and pain (for example, hot peppers!). These sensations combine with smells to create the total experience we call flavor. Flavor does more than make eating pleasant; it is also important to digestion. Stimulation of receptors in the nose and mouth triggers the release of the hormone insulin from the pancreas into the blood. Insulin regulates the body's use of sugar, which is used as fuel in the process of digestion.

A Chemical World

Human beings, like other animals, use odors to find food and avoid danger. Some researchers think we may also—unconsciously—use scent to select or attract a mate. We also recognize each other from odors. Blindfolded, mothers can find their babies in a crowded nursery using only their sense of smell. Husbands and wives can identify their spouses from the odor of their dirty shirts. Taste is important to survival, too. It can signal danger—nearly all natural poisons taste bitter—or trigger a feeling of well-being. The appeal of foods that taste good to us also helps to ensure that we will eat enough nutritious food to sustain life.

Tongue Maps: Fact or Fallacy?

Have you ever read that humans taste sweet at the front of the tongue and sour at the back? Maybe you have tried to map tastes on your tongue in science labs. If so, did you find it hard? "The tongue maps are wrong," says Yale University taste researcher Linda Bartoshuk. "The different tastes are detected all over the tongue."

However, not all tongues are created equal. Some people have more taste buds on their tongues than others, and some experience flavors more intensely, regardless of the number of taste buds. That's why everyone's taste is different.

Chapter **4**

Vision

We all say, "seeing is believing," but is that really accurate? At the University of Illinois, volunteers looked at a still picture on a TV screen. Whenever they moved their eyes or blinked, a computer automatically changed the picture in some way. Most people failed to notice the changes, even those as significant as a person disappearing from the scene. The researchers call this phenomenon "change blindness." Visual perception, it seems, is more a product of the brain than of the eye.

Eye and Brain

What color are your eyes? When you answer that question, you describe the colored ring of muscle called the iris. The iris contracts when light is dim. The contraction enlarges the pupil, which is the opening at the center of the iris. When the pupil is larger, it allows more light to enter. Behind the pupil lies a lens. It focuses light on the rear surface of the eye, the retina.

The retina contains a class of molecules called opsins. One such molecule, rhodopsin, is responsible for black and white vision. Rhodopsin contains the chemical retinal, a form of vitamin A. In the dark, retinal folds. When light strikes, it straightens. That change in shape sets off a series of chemical reactions. The reactions trigger a nerve impulse in your eyes' light receptors, which are called rods. Other forms of opsin do the same for color vision. They stimulate receptors called cones.

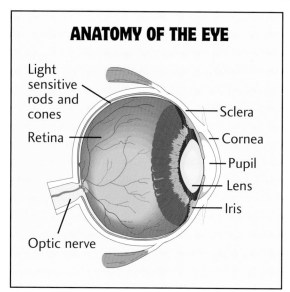

ANATOMY OF THE EYE

Light sensitive rods and cones

Retina

Optic nerve

Sclera

Cornea

Pupil

Lens

Iris

From the retina, impulses travel along one of two streams—the M stream or the P stream. The separation occurs in the retina's ganglion cells, which are the cell bodies of the optic nerves, and which receive and sort signals from many visual receptors. M and P ganglia transmit signals through two branches of the optic nerve.

The next stop for visual impulses is the thalamus. M signals travel faster and reach the thalamus first. These are the "where" signals that enable the brain to locate objects. The slower P signals last longer. They carry the "what" messages that enable the brain to identify what the object is. Fast-moving objects activate the M stream. Stationary objects and color send messages along the P path.

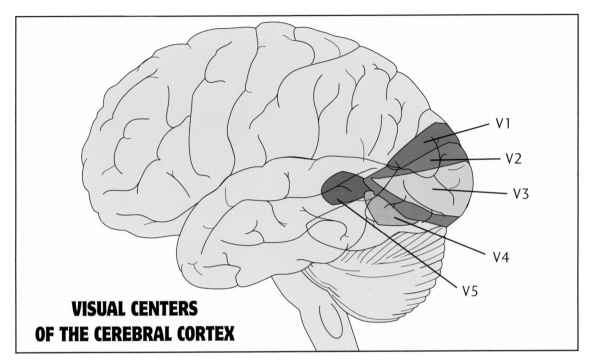

VISUAL CENTERS OF THE CEREBRAL CORTEX

From the thalamus, visual signals go to the primary visual cortex, or V1, at the back of the head. V1 neurons respond to very specific cues—such as lines and edges of objects—coming in from either eye. From V1, some signals travel to other centers called V2 and V4 before eventually being recognized as an object. Other signals travel from V1 through V2 and V3 on their way to V5. Neurons in the V5 respond to motion.

Six layers of neurons process visual information. In V1, V2, V5, and perhaps the other visual areas, the layers are stacked in columns, like coins. The columns respond to different kinds of input. Some detect only pinpoints of light; others, only edges and lines. They are so specialized that one line-detecting neuron "sees" only horizontal lines, while another picks up only edges a few degrees off the horizontal. Another detects only right angles.

How, then, can the brain recognize a complex stimulus such as your grandmother's face? No single neuron fires in response to a face. Instead, data about line, light, form, color, and motion all come together in certain areas of the cortex. There, neurons fire in response not to single inputs, but to patterns of input. That allows recognition of faces as distinct from other categories of objects, such as animals or vehicles or structures. Further processing links vision with memory, so that your grandmother's face can be identified as unique among all the faces that your brain has ever processed.

Moving Pictures

Close this book and scan its cover. How do you know that your eyes moved and not the book? If that question seems odd, remember that the same image will pass across the retina in either case.

Motion vision begins in the retina. There, M ganglia fire when they receive motion signals. Movement in a single direction stimulates some M cells. Movement in the opposite direction inhibits them, and they do not fire. In V1, input from many M cells comes together. They send signals directly to V5. Cells in V5 are organized in columns. The columns specialize in handling a particular direction of motion. Some columns fire when the background moves in a different direction from the viewer, as it did when you scanned the book cover. Those cells shut down and others fire when the background and the eyes move in the same direction, as they would if you watched a book fall from a table.

Color Vision

Light is a form of energy. It moves in waves. The distance between two tops (or two bottoms) of the waves is one wavelength. Different wavelengths of light create our perceptions of different colors. The retina's light receptors called cones respond to different wavelengths. "Blue cones" fire at wavelengths around 430 nanometers (abbreviated nm). [A nanometer is a billionth (1×10^{-9}) of a meter.] "Green cones" cover the 530-nm range. "Red cones" fire at around 560 nm.

The Moon Illusion

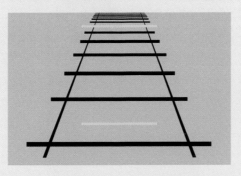

Optical illusions (perhaps better called brain illusions) are more than tricks or curiosities. They offer clues about how perception works.

The Ponzo illusion (above) is one example. The yellow bars are the same length, but the upper one looks longer. The brain assumes the "tracks" are parallel. Since the "distant" bar extends outside them, the brain "concludes" it must be longer.

To most people, the moon creates a similar illusion. It looks larger on the horizon than it does high in the sky. That perception is false. The moon is the same size and the same distance from the viewer whether it is low in the sky or high above.

Father-and-son team Lloyd and James Kaufman investigated the moon illusion. They projected moon images into the sky above a Long Island hilltop. Their subjects used a computer to place the images at a point they judged to be halfway between themselves and the moon. For the horizon moon, every subject estimated the halfway point farther away than for the overhead moon. As the Kaufmans' subjects moved either the horizon or a moon image closer, they said it looked smaller.

The Kaufmans think that objects on the ground make the moon look farther away. Because of this, the brain decides the moon must be bigger than it really is. When the moon rises high in the sky, distance cues are lost. Without them, the moon seems smaller.

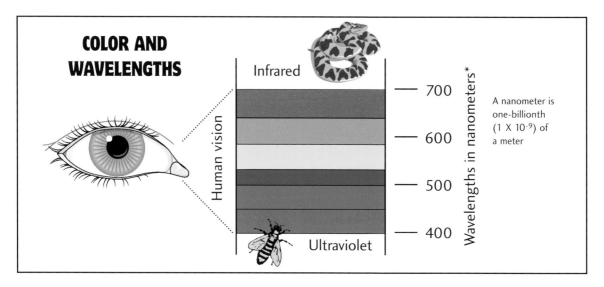

COLOR AND WAVELENGTHS

Infrared

Human vision

Wavelengths in nanometers*

— 700

— 600

— 500

— 400

Ultraviolet

A nanometer is one-billionth (1×10^{-9}) of a meter

Specialized cells in the retina's second layer "compare" the red, green, and blue signals and "compute" their balance. The V1 area of the cortex seems to lack color sensitivity, but V4 does a lot of color processing. Some scientists think the brain's ability to perceive color correctly, regardless of lighting conditions, lies in V4.

Have you ever noticed that your color vision fails at night? Everything looks black, white, or gray. That happens because cones respond only to color wavelengths. Rods, which handle black-and-white vision, outnumber cones ten to one. They are 1,000 times more sensitive than cones, making vision possible in dim light.

Filling In

What is the subject of the painting on page 37? The artist, Claude Monet, knew more about the brain than he may have realized. The brain's visual processing centers take minimal, subtle clues and interpret them broadly. In Monet's work, only a few colors and brush strokes are needed to send a clear message: "Water Lilies."

Adding information to complete a picture is called "filling in." When people glance at a patterned visual field that is missing a piece, they seldom consciously notice. To find out why, researchers studied cats. When the animals looked at a complete, patterned background, certain neurons in the V1 cortex fired. When the cats looked at the same pattern with a spot missing, the same V1 neurons fired. Neighboring neurons stimulated them.

Certain areas of the left and right sides of the brain specialize in the visual information they process. For example, scientists in London captured images of the brain at work while volunteers described either an overall pattern or a detail, such as a large "S" formed by a string of small "F's." The left brain worked most on the details, processing and recognizing the F's. The right brain processed the overall pattern, the S. The specialization of this recognition began in V2 and V3.

Depth and Distance

Human vision is binocular. That means both eyes register the same image at the same time, but from slightly different angles.

Monet's painting only "suggests" the subject; our brains "fill in" the rest.

The brain uses the angular differences to create a three-dimensional view, or perspective of where the object is in space. To get an idea how this works, go to the next page. Place an index card between the girl and the flag above. Lower your head until the card touches your nose and forehead. What happens?

BINOCULAR VISION

As you move closer to the page, the flag moves closer to the girl so that eventually she appears to be holding it.

Your eyes rotate inward (cross slightly) to see close objects clearly. They swing wider apart to focus at a distance. Muscles around the eyes change the angle of view. The muscles of the lens also contract, flattening it to focus on near objects and rounding it for distant objects. The brain uses information from both sets of muscles to judge distance.

Clues from the environment also aid in perceiving depth and distance. If one of two objects known to be the same size looks smaller, the brain assumes it must be farther away. Or if distance clues suggest one of the objects is farther away, the brain assumes it must be larger. These assumptions can sometimes trick the brain, leading it to false conclusions.

A World of Light

The brain does not always perceive visual stimuli accurately. One reason is the two-way flow of information between the brain's visual centers and areas in the parietal cortex that focus attention. Attention impulses control the selection of inputs. They tell the visual areas what to process and what to ignore. For example, when researchers asked people to pay attention to both color and movement, the subjects' color-processing and V5 regions grew active. When asked to watch only for a change in color, the V5 areas stayed quiet.

Studies such as these demonstrate the important difference between "looking" with the eyes and "seeing" with the brain.

More Brain Illusions

The brain uses many clues to perceive depth and distance. It also assumes many things that are not necessarily true.

Clue	How It Works
Blocking or overlapping	An object that partially blocks another object must be closer.
Brightness	Surfaces farther from a light source appear darker. (The shadows tell you this apple is round.)
Sharp focus	Closer objects appear clear. Those at a distance blur.
Size of image on retina	The larger the image, the nearer the object seems.
Elevation	Distant objects appear higher than those nearby.
Texture	We see less detail in distant objects than in near ones. (You can discern individual leaves on trees that are near, but those in the distance look like splashes of green.)
Perspective	Distant objects look closer together than near ones.
Motion	Near objects appear to move more rapidly than distant ones. (A train appears to move faster than a plane.)

Chapter 5

Hearing

A bell rings. Its sound comes from a valley to the south. The pitch of its strike tone is a perfect middle C. The listener far away cannot see the bell, but the existence of the bell is certain. Hearing informs the brain that it is so.

Hearing and vision are alike in several ways. Sound is vibration—pressure moving in waves. In air, it moves in surges, like a Slinky toy. The human brain interprets wavelengths of light as color. It perceives wavelengths of sound as pitch.

Vision is binocular (two eyes). It helps the brain locate objects and judge their distance. Hearing is binaural (two ears). Information coming into two ears lets the brain locate the source and the distance of sound.

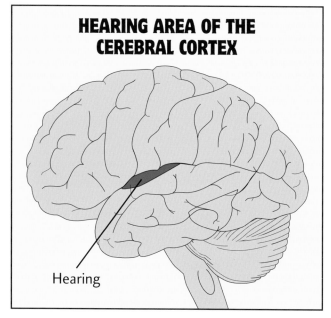

HEARING AREA OF THE CEREBRAL CORTEX

Hearing

Vision has two separate neural pathways to the brain: one for "what" and one for "where." Hearing has "what" and "where" paths, too. They run to primary auditory processing areas in the cerebral cortex, located at the sides of the head above the ears.

Pitch and Timbre

Sound vibrations travel through air as alternating waves of high and low pressure. As a wave travels, each molecule in the air vibrates because it receives some energy from its nearest neighbor. At high pressure, the molecules crowd together. At low pressure, they spread apart. The distance between two high pressures or two low pressures is one wavelength.

Sound is described by its frequency. That is the number of pressure waves that vibrate back and forth in one second. That unit of frequency is the Hertz (Hz). One Hertz is one complete vibration in one second.

The shorter the wavelength, the greater the frequency and the higher the pitch. For a high pitch, think of a soprano or a piccolo compared to the low pitch of a baritone or a tuba. Humans can detect frequencies between 20 and 20,000 Hertz. Our greatest sensitivity lies in the 1,000–5,000 Hertz region. Most speech falls between 200 and 8,000 Hz.

Most sounds are a mixture of frequencies. They are modified by such factors as the resonance of the vibrating material and the echoes off surfaces in the environment. When mixed signals enter the auditory system, the brain perceives each one separately. That helps differentiate sounds. For example, the pure tone of middle-C is 256 Hz, but the middle C strike tone of a bell sounds different from middle C on a piano. This property of a sound source is called timbre.

Loudness

Intensity is a property of a sound wave. It is how much energy the sound wave has. Pluck a guitar string gently and you produce a sound of lower intensity than if you pluck it hard. The human brain perceives intensity as loudness. In general, sounds of greater intensity sound louder. However, the perception of loudness depends on distance and pitch. The farther away the listener, the less intense the sound. And it takes greater intensity to make a low-pitched tone sound as loud as a high-pitched one.

Sound intensity is measured in decibels (dB). A soft whisper registers around 30 decibels. People speak at about 60 dB. An automobile at 25 feet (about 8 meters) away hums at 80dB, while a blender whirs at 90. Jackhammers, guns, airplanes, and sirens produce sounds in the 120–140 dB range. That is loud enough to damage the ear, and people near them must use protective devices. Amplification at rock concerts commonly increases the intensity of the music to 120 dB or more, which can cause permanent ear damage.

Generally, a sound of ten times greater intensity is perceived as twice as loud. That means it takes ten cheerleaders to achieve twice the volume of one cheerleader. The difference between "barely audible" and "painful" is a 10 trillion times (1×10^{13}) increase in intensity.

WAVELENGTHS AND FREQUENCY

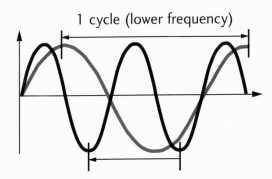

The black and red waves here have different frequencies. The frequency of the red wave is half that of the black, and, consequently, its pitch is an octave lower.

Amplified rock music is often loud enough to cause hearing damage to listeners.

People perceive sounds as louder than they actually are because the human ear increases their intensity. Vibration of bones in the head along with vibrations of air and fluid in the ear passage—amplify sound. In the 2,000 to 4,000 Hz range, the increase may be as great as 10 to 15 dB. The lever-action of tiny bones attached to the eardrum can amplify sound by as much as 25 decibels.

Ear and Brain

The part of your ear that you see in your mirror is really a collection device. It collects and concentrates sound waves. The waves vibrate air inside your auditory canal. The air then passes the vibration along to the eardrum. A tiny bone is attached to the inside of the eardrum. It is called the hammer because of its shape. It is connected to two other bones—the anvil and the stirrup—also named for their shapes.

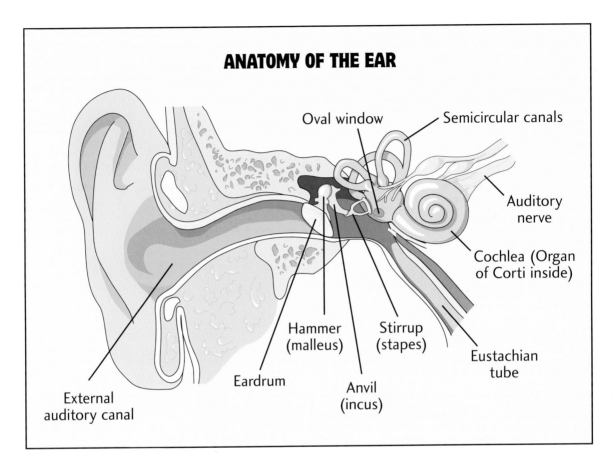

ANATOMY OF THE EAR

Oval window
Semicircular canals
Auditory nerve
Cochlea (Organ of Corti inside)
Hammer (malleus)
Stirrup (stapes)
Eardrum
Anvil (incus)
Eustachian tube
External auditory canal

The stirrup joins a structure on the spiral-shaped cochlea called the oval window. Below the oval window lies another flexible membrane, called the round window. The vibration of the stirrup causes the oval window to vibrate. When the oval window pushes in, the round window moves out, and vice versa. High-pitched sounds with short wavelengths cause the oval and round windows to vibrate rapidly. Low-pitched sounds cause slower vibrations.

Vibration of the oval window causes movement of fluid inside the cochlea. There lies the true receptor of sound, the Organ of Corti. On it lie some 15,000 to 20,000 hair cells, each with as many as 100 tiny hairs projecting from it. The hairs move when the basilar membrane (attached to the Organ of Corti) vibrates.

The hair movement causes chemical changes, which, in turn, change electrical potential. Nerve impulses begin.

The arrangement of hair cells on the basilar membrane controls the perception of pitch. High-pitched sounds produce the greatest movement near the oval window. Here, the membrane is thin and stiff. The hair cells in this area are most sensitive to high pitches. Farther inside the cochlea, the membrane grows thicker and softer. The hair cells in that area fire in response to lower frequency vibrations.

Some 30,000 nerve fibers lead from the Organ of Corti to the auditory nerve. That nerve carries impulses from the ear to the part of the brain where sound impulses are separated into components—including frequency and intensity—for further processing. The thalamus acts as a relay station for hearing, as it does for all the senses except smell. It discards some signals and transmits others. The selective action of the thalamus is essential to hearing. Its action, for example, explains how people who live near an airport eventually stop noticing the constant roar of take-offs and landings.

Separate impulses travel from the thalamus to the auditory processing centers of the cortex. The major sound-processing region is called the auditory cortex.

Processing

One of the first structures in the brain to process sound is called the inferior colliculus. Its lower part is a place where impulses from the two ears come together and are checked for differences in timing and strength. Higher up, neurons are organized in layers, or sheets. The sheets respond to different sound frequencies.

The inferior colliculus also responds to how long a sound lasts. Such processing allows the brain to distinguish words, such as "to" and "do." They have the same mix of frequencies, but the initial sound in "to" lasts about a millisecond (1/1000th of a second) longer.

Timing differences also help to pinpoint the location of sounds. Neurons in the inferior colliculus send timing impulses to the auditory cortex. There, neurons "compute" the difference in the time it takes sounds to arrive in each ear. The difference in the intensity of waves reaching the two ears also helps to locate where the sound is coming from. Moving sound stimulates the auditory area on the brain's right side. This is the brain's "where" processor for sound.

The auditory cortex maps frequencies very precisely. Neurons in orderly columns fire in response to different pitches. The outer areas of the auditory cortex handle high-pitched sounds. Lower pitches are processed deeper in the cortex. Certain areas of the auditory cortex are especially sensitive to complex sounds and rhythmic patterns.

One specialized area separates meaningful sounds from background noise. At a party, you can converse with a person near you, while the talk all around you sounds like a muffled buzz. But if someone on the other side of the room speaks your name, you hear it clearly. Scientists call that the "foreground-background decomposition" function of the auditory cortex.

Auditory processing areas in the brain are linked closely to attention-focusing areas and to short-term memory storage. For a fraction of a second, the brain remembers everything it hears. Just behind the auditory cortex lies an area where longer-term sound memories are stored. This area allows the brain to distinguish a birdcall from a tolling bell. Spoken language has its own pathways. Speech centers on the brain's left side, near the auditory cortex, attach meaning to words. The right side interprets tones of voice and senses the emotions that underlie words. These are the brain's "what" pathways for speech sounds.

A World of Sound

Just as no single visual neuron recognizes your grandmother's face, no single auditory neuron "knows" a bell or a sound

HUMAN VS. ANIMAL HEARING

Human hearing is sharp, but our ability to detect high-pitched sounds is poor compared to many other animals.

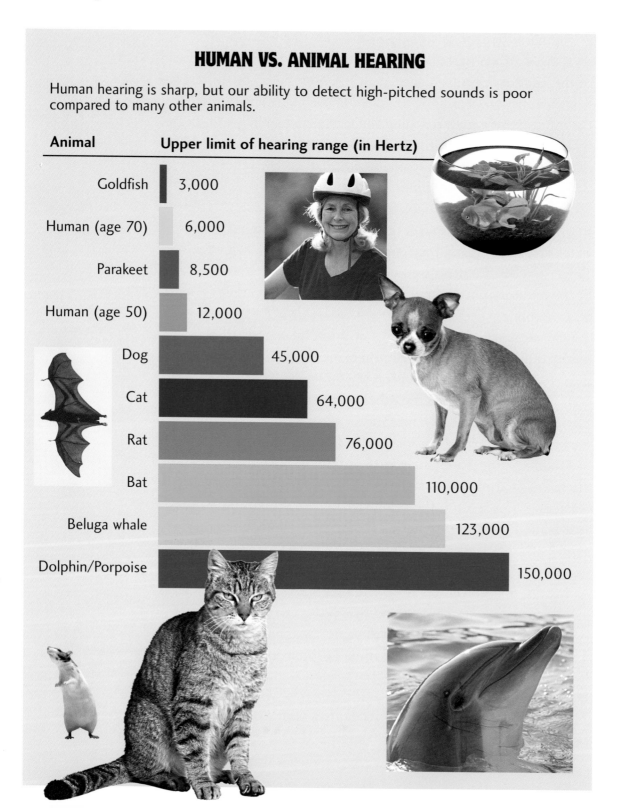

Animal	Upper limit of hearing range (in Hertz)
Goldfish	3,000
Human (age 70)	6,000
Parakeet	8,500
Human (age 50)	12,000
Dog	45,000
Cat	64,000
Rat	76,000
Bat	110,000
Beluga whale	123,000
Dolphin/Porpoise	150,000

coming from the south or your grand-mother's voice. Ellen Covey, who studies hearing at the University of Washington, says individual neurons act like microscopic computers, compiling information and making choices. "In hearing, the brain does not function as one big computer," she says, "but rather as a series of small computers working in series and in parallel."

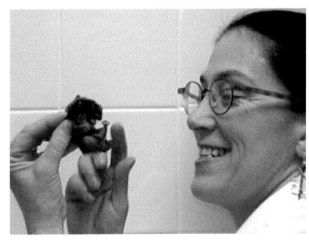

Ellen Covey studies hearing at the University of Washington. She uses brown bats for many of her subjects.

Covey studies the auditory system of the North American big brown bat, which is similar to that of humans. She uses tiny glass electrodes to record the electrical activity of the bats' brains. Some sounds excite brain cells, making them more likely to respond to a signal. Other sounds inhibit neurons, making them less likely to respond. Covey says bats' brains "compute" the patterns of excited and inhibited cells in determining what a sound is and where it is coming from.

Perhaps humans do the same when they hear a bell . . . ringing south of here . . . at perfect middle C.

6

Balance and Motion

Y ou run to the park with a group of your best skateboarding friends. There, you take your board to the top of the ramp. You assess height, angle, and position. Then you step on the board and—whoa!—you're zooming down the curve and back up again. As you hit the end of the curve, you and your board take off into the air. You soar for a moment and then land perfectly on the ground below. Your friends all cheer. You were awesome.

Skateboarding requires many of your senses to work all at once. It also involves some senses you may never have thought much about.

Your brain controls posture, balance, and motion as you move through your world each day. It coordinates such actions as jumping, running, and landing upright. As you fly through the air on a skateboard, you are aware of many things at once. You know that you are you. That "sense of self," or consciousness, is the most powerful and puzzling sense of all.

Time and Cycles

Most living things follow a precisely timed schedule of daily, monthly, and yearly changes. Internal clocks control the daily periods of activity and rest, and the longer life cycles of growth, development, and reproduction.

How do body clocks work? Michael Young at Rockefeller University studies the chemicals in cells that produce daily rhythms in fruit flies. In the dark, a substance called TIM accumulates in their eyes and in "pacemaker cells" in their brains. In the light, TIM breaks down rapidly. Young can shift the fruit flies' daily cycles by advancing or delaying light periods, thus changing the amounts of TIM in their eyes and brains. Substances similar to TIM are found in all animals, and they probably have similar functions.

In humans, the body's internal clock lies in the SCN (suprachiasmatic nucleus) of the hypothalamus. This cluster of about 10,000 neurons regulates sleep, hunger, and body temperature. (Did you know that you cool slightly at night?) The SCN controls the production and release of the hormone melatonin from the pineal gland. Melatonin levels rise at night and fall during the day.

The human biological clock keeps ticking even in complete darkness, but light can "reset" it. That is why jet travelers can adapt to new time zones within a few days. Human eyes contain proteins called cryptochromes. (They are different from the opsins that trigger visual impulses.) The cryptochromes are linked to vitamin B-2. Many scientists think that changes in cryptochromes send messages to the SCN that keep the body clock synchronized with the environment.

Balance and Motion

Structures deep inside the ear help the brain monitor and maintain balance and posture. Three loop-shaped, fluid-filled tubes send the brain the information it needs to perceive movement. These semicircular canals lie at right angles to each other. Body movement in any direction starts waves inside them. The waves move tiny hairs at the ends of the canals. The hairs send impulses to the brain. The result of these impulses is the sense of motion that tells the brain what the body is doing—whether it is walking, running, or turning a cartwheel.

As is important with cartwheels, the brain also needs to know whether the body is right side up, upside down, or tilted. Between the semicircular canals and the cochlea lies a chamber about the size of your little finger-nail. Inside it are two tiny sacs. The membranes of these sacs contain grains of minerals called otoliths. Also inside the sacs are hair cells. When the body changes position, the otoliths "fall," as would any stone in Earth's gravity. Their movement brings them in contact with the hair cells. Impulses sent from the hair cells tell the brain how the body is positioned in space.

Structures deep inside the ear help the brain monitor posture, movement, and balance.

The motor cortex of the cerebrum triggers the muscle actions that cause voluntary movement, such as jumping up to grab hold of the monkey bars. A supplementary motor cortex plans voluntary actions before they are carried out. The cerebellum coordinates sensory inputs and motor commands. The control of habitual movements, such as going down stairs, shifts to the cerebellum. The cerebellum allows new skills—such as riding a bicycle or driving a car—to eventually become "automatic" with practice.

The Phantom Foot

Look at the pictures to the right. Is picture A a right foot or a left foot? What about picture B? Which question was easier to answer? Can you think of a reason why?

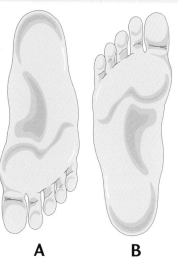

A   **B**

they called A.Z. Born without arms below the elbow or legs below the groin, her brain nonetheless solved the left/right foot problem the same way people with limbs do. She mentally rotated an image of a foot she never had. Imaging studies showed activity in the same parts of A.Z.'s brain that people with limbs use to move their arms and legs.

If you are like most people, you answer by rotating your mental image of your foot into the positions shown. Question B is easier than A because the foot is turned in the same direction as your body. You have less imaginary rotating to do.

Where did that mental image of your foot come from? Research has shown that people born without hands, arms, legs, or feet can have the same sensation of limbs as people who are born with them.

In 2000, Swiss scientists reported on brain imaging studies of a woman

How A.Z.'s perception of limbs developed is unknown, but the researchers think that imitation may be involved. When studying animals, scientists see the same brain areas at work whether the animal moves its own hand or watches another animal move its hand. Researchers guess that A.Z.'s body image developed as she observed movement in others.

Not all the regulators of movement are in the brain. Lift this book, and your muscles automatically exert the proper amount of force—no less and no more. At full contraction, muscles can exert enough force to damage joints. Force detectors in the muscles and joints prevent overcontraction, so that a simple action such as lifting a book does not rip a muscle from its attachment.

Force detectors in the muscles and joints automatically prevent muscles from ripping out of their attachments.

But what if a set of encyclopedias unexpectedly falls into your arms? Your body protects itself against sudden force with a response so important that no time is wasted sending signals to the brain. The myotatic (stretch) reflex occurs because a sensory neuron sends an impulse to the spinal cord. Immediately, a motor neuron in the spinal cord sends back a message, ordering, "Contract!" This instantaneous shortening prevents the muscle from pulling too far. The myotatic reflex is the tension you feel when you stretch. It is also the reason your lower leg jerks when the doctor taps your knee with a rubber mallet.

Some of the control mechanisms for muscles are built in. For example, when a motor neuron fires causing the contraction of a skeletal muscle, it stimulates things called Renshaw cells. These cells inhibit the firing of the very motor neuron that stimulated them. Without them, the contraction would cause more neuronal firing, and the neuronal firing would cause more contraction. The endless cycle of ever-greater contraction would eventually destroy the muscle. Renshaw cells break the cycle and let the muscle relax when its work is done.

Chapter 7

The Human Experience

Perception. One word means so much. Perception is about detecting the nature of both outer and inner worlds. In many cases, it also means responding in some way, either consciously or unconsciously.

The five basic senses—sight, hearing, touch, taste, and smell—collect and process data on light, sound, pressure, pain, and chemicals. The senses of movement and body position respond to gravity and muscle contraction. But think how much farther your senses go. Vision, for example, identifies objects in the environment and primes the systems that maintain posture and balance in the face of obstacles. You step over a curb and around a tree without a thought. The response is automatic.

Vision creates perceptions that are even more complex. For example, the sight of human facial expressions and the sound of language inflection combine to tell us what others are thinking and feeling. How does the brain link facial expression to emotions? To find out, one team of scientists studied people who had brain damage in areas that process touch, pain, and temperature impulses from the skin. The people could not infer (figure out and process) what another person's mental state was from looking at that person's facial expressions. "To figure out how someone feels from looking at their face requires us to imagine what it would feel like if we made that same face," says Ralph Adolphs, a researcher at the University of Iowa.

Since 1990, scientists have discovered more about the senses and perception than was previously known in all the centuries before. Still, much remains to be learned about the marvelous and mysterious brain.

Life and Living

Not all brain research seeks to cure disease or heal injuries. Much of the knowledge scientists seek can be applied to everyday life. For example, when Robert Zatorre of McGill University in Montreal wanted to see how the brain perceives music, he turned to a technique called PET (positron emission tomography). PET images detect oxygen as it concentrates in the most active areas of the brain.

When his volunteers listened to simple tunes, their brains "lit up" on the right side, roughly opposite to the language-processing centers on the left side. To his surprise, he also found increased activity in the brain's visual centers, at the back of the head. Does the brain "see" pitch as movement up and down the scale? Does music evoke visual images deep in our brains? These questions not only intrigue Zatorre, but also hundreds of other researchers around the world.

Technology

Research into the senses has many applications. For example, University of Illinois scientists have developed an "artificial nose" that "sees" smells. "The human nose is generally sensitive to most compounds at a level of a few parts per million," says chemist Kenneth Suslick. "The sensitivity of our artificial nose is 10 to 100 times better than the human nose for many compounds."

Recent research has shown that music stimulates the brain's visual centers as well as the auditory centers.

The researchers put dots of many different dyes on a piece of paper, plastic, or glass. Each type of airborne molecule reacts with the dyes in a unique way. "By subtracting the 'before' image from the 'after' image, we obtain the color-change pattern of the odorant," says Suslick. Called "smell-seeing" by its inventors, the technique offers promise for detecting tiny amounts of environmental pollutants, poisonous gases, illegal drugs, or toxins. It may also be used to prevent food spoilage.

Consciousness

Is a body necessary to the perception, "I am me"? How does your brain define you as separate from—but a part of—the world around you?

Some basics are built into brains from birth. For example, infants look longer at new stimuli than at familiar ones. This ability to perceive objects as real and interesting requires no learning. It is present before babies reach for things.

Part of consciousness is a "sense of self" in time. Humans perceive themselves as different—but still themselves—in the past, present, and future. Some brain injuries rob the consciousness of that sense. For example, some people suffer from severe amnesia (loss of memory). These people live constantly in the present. They can neither remember nor imagine anything past or future.

Some philosophers have defined consciousness as "awareness of awareness." You are aware of yourself and all that is around you. You are aware that you are aware. You can have an internal conversation with yourself, imagining events that may not happen or actions that you may not take. Is consciousness that internal dialogue? How does the brain create and sustain it? These are questions that scientists, as well as theologians and philosophers, have been trying to answer for centuries.

Part of being "human" is the ability to perceive abstract concepts, such as loyalty, courage, and honor.

Consciousness may be more than an awareness of being aware. The ability to imagine people, events, or situations is based in reality—it is an extension of things we actually experience. The perception, however, of abstract concepts, such as truth or honor, requires imagining something that does not exist in the physical world. Human beings cannot see, hear, taste, touch, or smell qualities such as faith, justice, or integrity, but they can define them, value them, and base their actions on them. To the human brain, the concepts of loyalty, compassion, and candor are as real as hunger pangs or breakfast bacon. That is just one of the things that makes our brains so incredibly complex and unique.

The "Cosmic Questions" of Perception

Finally, scientists are beginning to tackle, as never before, the questions once considered purely the domain of philosophers. The human brain fragments our world into bits of data. Why, then, do we experience the world in a unified way? Why, indeed, is there experience at all? Being able to even think about the answer to this question makes you (and all humans) unique. Answering this question one day might be one of the greatest feats any brain could accomplish.

For More Information

BOOKS

Barbor, Marcus. *The Human Brain.* Philadelphia, PA: Running Press, 1999. Includes a model to build.

Byles, Monica and William Wharfe. *Senses.* New York: World Book, 2000. Includes CD-ROM.

Cobb, Vicki. *How to Really Fool Yourself: Illusions for All Your Senses.* New York: John Wiley, 1999.

Friedhoffer, Robert. *Magic and Perception: The Art and Science of Fooling the Senses.* New York: Franklin Watts, 1996.

Hartley, Karen; Chris MacRo and Philip Taylor. *The Sixth Sense and Other Special Senses.* New York: Heinemann Library, 2000.

Llamas, Andreu. *The Nervous System.* Milwaukee, WI: Gareth Stevens, 1998.

Llinas, Rodolfo (editor). *Workings of the Brain: Development, Memory, and Perception.* New York: Econo-Clad Books, 1999.

MacRo, Karen Hartley (editor), Chris MacRo, and Philip Taylor. *The Senses Series: Hearing in Living Things; Seeing in Living Things; Smelling in Living Things; Tasting in Living Things;*
Touching in Living Things. New York: Heinemann Library, 2000.

Miller-Schroeder, Patricia. *The Science of Senses.* Milwaukee, WI: Gareth Stevens, 2000.

Parker, Steve. *Senses.* Brookfield, CT: Copper Beech Books, 1997.

Rowan, Peter. *Big Head!* New York: Knopf, 1998.

WEB SITES

Brain Basics Learn more about how the brain works and how to keep it healthy— www.ninds.nih.gov/health_and_medical/ pubs/brain_basics_know_your_brain.htm

Brain Collections Compare the brains of different mammals—http://brainmuseum.org/

Brain Tour Take a tour of the brain, as well as find information about the history of the study of the brain— http://suhep.phy.syr.edu/courses/modules/ MM/Biology/biology.html

Seeing, Hearing, and Smelling the World Find more information about the human senses. This Web site features many colorful diagrams— www.hhmi.org/senses/start.htm

Glossary

Axon The long, thin strand that carries impulses away from the cell body of a neuron.

Cerebellum The area of the brain that controls many aspects of movement, including balance and learned skills.

Cerebrum The majority of the human brain, divided by a fissure into the right and left hemispheres.

Cerebral cortex In humans, the thin outer layer of the cerebrum responsible for most higher-level thought and sensory perception.

Cochlea The spiral-shaped organ in the
inner ear where sound impulses are generated.

Cone A light receptor in the eye responsible for color vision.

Cryptochromes Chemicals in the eye that may send light signals to "set" the body's internal clock.

Decibel The unit of measure of the intensity of sound.

Dendrite A thin branch typically shorter than an axon that carries impulses toward the cell body of a neuron.

Frequency The number of wavelengths (of

sound) per unit time.

Ganglion cells Neurons in the eye that collect impulses from a large number of receptors.

Hertz The unit of measurement for sound wave frequency.

Hippocampus A part of the limbic system in the human brain associated with the formation of new memories. *See also* amygdala.

Hormone A chemical secreted from one organ that travels through the bloodstream to another organ, where it produces some effect.

Hypothalamus A gland in the brain that secretes hormones.

Inferior colliculus A sound processing structure in the brain.

Limbic system Several structures inside the brain that control some basic life functions, manage emotions, and promote formation of new memories.

Motor neuron A neuron that carries an impulse from the brain or spinal cord to a muscle, where it stimulates contraction.

Nerve cell See neuron.

Nerve fiber Any one of the many bundles of neurons that link the brain and spinal cord with the rest of the body.

Neuron A cell that carries the nerve impulse, consisting of a cell body, an axon, and dendrites.

Neurotransmitter Any one of 150 or more chemicals released from an axon that crosses the synapse and initiates an impulse in another neuron; more generally, any naturally-produced chemical that affects the action of the brain or nervous system.

Olfactory nerve The major nerve fiber that carries impulses from the nose to the brain.

Opsins A class of chemicals found in the retina that changes shape in the light and triggers impulses in rods and cones.

Optic nerve The major nerve fiber that carries impulses from the eye to the brain.

Organ of Corti Structure in the cochlea that generates nerve impulses in response to specific pitches (frequencies).

Otolith A tiny mineral grain in the sacs of the inner ear that helps the brain keep the body balanced.

PET (Positron Emission Tomography) A method of imaging the brain and other internal organs using radioactive tracers to identify regions of increased glucose or oxygen use.

Pitch The frequency of sound vibrations.

Pituitary A gland that secretes and releases hormones under direction from the hypothalamus.

Prostaglandins Chemicals involved in inflammation and the perception of pain.

Pupil The opening through the iris that allows light to enter the eye.

Receptor (sensory) A sensory neuron that fires in response to a stimulus (mechanical, chemical, light, or other).

Reflex arc The direct response of a motor neuron in the spinal cord to an impulse from a sensory neuron, producing an immediate, involuntary action.

Retina The structure at the back of the eye that contains light receptors.

Rhodopsin A chemical in the retina that changes shape in response to light and initiates an impulse in a light-sensing neuron.

Rod A light receptor in the eye responsible for black and white vision.

SCN An area of the hypothalamus that maintains the body's clock.

Second messenger A molecule produced by a neuron that initiates a nerve impulse.

Semicircular canals Organs of balance in the inner ear.

Sensory neuron A nerve cell that carries an impulse from a sense organ to the brain or spinal cord.

Sound Waves of high and low pressure in a medium (e. g. air or water).

Substance P A chemical involved in inflammation and the perception of pain.

Thalamus A structure in the brain that serves as a relay station for all sensory information except smell.

Timbre The quality of a sound, influenced by its source, resonance, and echoes, and pitch and intensity.

Index